Dream-beauty-psycho

Todd Swift

Dream-beauty-psycho

NEW POEMS

 EYEWEAR PUBLISHING

First published in 2017
by Eyewear Publishing Ltd
Suite 333, 19-21 Crawford Street
Marylebone, London W1H 1PJ
United Kingdom

Typeset with graphic design by Edwin Smet
Cover photograph by Todd Swift, of his wife Sara, at the Barbican
Printed in England by TJ International Ltd, Padstow, Cornwall

ISBN 978-1-911335-91-7

Eyewear wishes to thank Jonathan Wonham for his generous patronage of our press.

WWW.EYEWEARPUBLISHING.COM

THIS BOOK IS DEDICATED TO
SARA AND SUETONIUS.

TABLE OF CONTENTS

BOWIE

(i.m.)

strangeness
often unfamiliar
not you
you did newness

as if difference
was equal
and oddness true
art your skin

song your suit
masks your nakedness
change your dress
it was never love

alone or sex
or even intoxication
there was constant
revolution in orbit

with you from ignition
as if dating
a calendar burning time
as it recited modernity

in angular rhyme
terrifying cold
hot and blue Duke
queen and alien weirdly

crossed in one form
you danced on norms
until beauty became a fluke
to resurrect Berlin

HOT HOUR

It's the hot hour
after the heat,
and doubt is humid
in my area. I fear,

suddenly, our small family,
an Us at last –
only a kitten, some parents
might tut –

but the thirdness brings
joy in the linking
of two to speak of another,
to love another

in the lost house.
Do not go, days
of my gentle love, cycling
home in brown gloves.

We are still ourselves,
even older, but I sense
a breaking of a season
over the rooftops,

the clouds musky. Time
builds, it does, it does,
until it breaks, a sort
of climacteric. O love

I recognise, latterly, late
your blessedness.
Hold our slight Suetonius
in unasking sleep.

IN THE LOBBY

he asked where are you going
and why is your left
trouser pocket singed?

his father who was a singer
said he was going
for water and the matchbook

in his pocket had turned
to fire under the tight
press of thigh and material.

i see the son replied,
sad about the burning smell,
and thoughts of having died

and gone to hell uppermost
in his concerned mind,
but otherwise, are you well?

why do you ask?
his father said. because
your office was turned

into a crèche for children
ten years ago father,
look around you.

he did. am I in the ground?
he queried. no, you
are in heaven,

because we can meet
like this after so long.
yes, he said, returning

to hear a loved one's living
voice is higher song. then,
after the refrain was gone.

FOR SARA IN BLACKROCK

The walk at dark
along the seafront
back to your home
after many years
married, at winter's
low tide, solstice,
was a new game
being played
but hark! the brunt
of lapsed hours
when vows were lost
at sea all came good
like a lottery ticket
worn too long
in the old coat
of your father, found
like the deepest shark,
pulled out with tobacco;
too tattered to be
redeemed for the win
itself, but a Nevertheless
rushes out of the find
that some fortunate
recollections live up
to the full bursts of promise
to set time up
for a welcome fall
into the bed of making,
the winding sheets of the sea
that coast on being lovers.

COHEN DIES, THEN TRUMP WINS

(i.m. l.c.)

I.
Canadiana was toppled by a man
Who wore his sly fedora

Like a battle plan; devastating
Gloom a glamour, darkness

Sitting for one's kin; the Klan
That burns the heartless crosses

Is the one that lost their oars;
You drift to shore on ignorance

Once the battle hymn's been sung,
The stars and stripes torn apart.

Yon future's thrown to reckless
Abandon, gone to seed in word

And Abaddon, as if the Holy Bible
Was a blueprint for building sin.

His feckless crew threw their captain
To low sharks, then set high masts

Aglow with gasoline; hijinks musicked
To the light of a damaged moon.

The ship of state is sick, C Manson
A sad maidenhead and DJ Trump

Playing relentless simplicity,
Hate's pitiable tunes; victory

Is another way of destroying
What one hates to be;

Vaster Reality got sucked out
Like a bad yolk long ago.

2.
I loved Cohen and I hated him
In equal measures of age

And lust; he was the victim
Suffering less with each great moan;

He was the rag and bone guy
Strumming a ghetto violin;

The ash of his ancestors drifting
Like Frost's snowy evening,

But this was the ghoulish milk of
Weimar evil plucking every string;

No trusted cantor ever sings
Without a sense of G-D;

Senseless to bring lyricism
To a fragile world otherwise

Than in darkening optimism;
Now, lights are out across

The plains, and Abraham
Has taken the glinting promise

To the prominent vein;
Our sons of freedom bleed

Their bright longing meanness
And the daughters are betrayed;

Grand old republic, singed Ilium,
The half-clad emperor is abed

After sleeping with the soldiery;
And Leonard the lover is dead.

Undead, like Lugosi, in his tomb,
Restless like Lincoln

While the batwings bloom,
And the need for ever-urgent

Loving continues its slow pace
Of opiated gentleness, gathering.

Bless the gentile and the Jew,
The many and the few,

The small and the elite,
The manly and effete,

But love what is higher than true;
That good pours out of heaven

It spills and slips, uneven.
And pours back into you.

LESBIAN VAMPIRE ACADEMY

It is not, one might suspect, a place for sisters
To swallow a garlic tablet, or inspect a crucifix;

Lipstick applied strictly without mirrors;
The librarian expects Swinburne's books

Returned to the minute or penalties accrue;
Turned at eighteen from mortal to undivine,

They prefer their correction on the rack
Wriggling as they divest them of mortal wine –

The inside gag they have to label our blood –
For make no mistake, these fanged co-eds

With their skirts and blouses kill for sport
Like gods did once; they're the new thing,

Digitally connected to the boys they lure
To suspend upside down, pleading anaemia

Or malaria or worse – girls long in tooth,
Their claws decreased for Instagram, their busts

Instead pronounced – most from Romantic
Lands, or so they sound – they smirk, and grind

Their words like chewing bones, torture
Syntax because they can; whip their torsos

Into archaic shape, and shine at night
As brightly as any chemical tan applied;

I have begged for these daughters of Satan
To accept me onto their course; their syllabi

Defeats most sibyls, their demonic kissing
Transformative as any degree in engineering

Or genetics. I want to learn to die in the arms
Of one of these creatures of the evening glow –

Though they prefer artifice and gaming
Among their own lithe immortal jejune kind;

They toss and throw men around like dice,
Break off their parts like icicles in red snow;

And genuinely disdain what jets from lust
Except it has glucose and drips roseate,

Sublimely, from a gashed open vein or more;
Don't call them tarts or harlots or whores,

Just because you cannot control their feeding
Or what drives them to desire a frenzied milk

That runs in rivulets down the giving dead.
I ask for them to have mercy on my Christian

Birth and imbue me with acrobatic skills
So I can fly-crawl and web-scuttle as they do;

I have been led here by graphic insights
And a craving to live when rivals pass away;

But tonight is Halloween so they are gay
And dancing sickly-pale, half-vivid, quiet

To hear the ringing of girls from the academy
Trick or treating in the laneway; I am dropped

Like a bad option and told to return next year.
I pass giggling donors dressed as ghosts,

Envision soaked engaging toasts ahead;
Praying to the grape-ripe moon for dark power.

30 October, 2015

THE CAT

AFTER BAUDELAIRE'S POEM (after Jan Owen's version)

In my head he prowls
like in our flat,
gorgeous cat: strong, soft,
charismatic; when he mews
we barely hear, because
his voice is soft too.
But his purring is another
story, then he's profoundly

noticed like any rich baron.
He throws his presence around
in growls and that deep sound,
the trick a good cat knows.
His purrs can claw
right into my shadowy self
that otherwise prefers to hide.
He is an incisive guy.

The knowledge he's with me
in the gloom, the dark room,
is a blaze of song,
the best poem or opium.
I sometimes am sedated by him.
That trembling emblematic
outpour from my feline buddy
defeats evil, defines goodness.

No distress when he's in my bed.
Words are outmoded
compared to his output.
His ouevre is deep and wide
without the fuss of art.
My mystery cat, my friend
at night, at play, my lovely
cat of cats, your orchestral

scores are genius beyond
Mozart, because your vocality
thrums within and across
the full being of you, ball
of fur and curious harmony.
Angels have what you've got,
but are less real, and don't curl
on my chest as I sleep or weep.

Paris, 2016

THE BASTARDS

The new bastards took over
From the old bastards

Who all now agree
Had been better bastards

All things considered.
The new bastards

Were actually evil bastards.
Thugs of the type

We last saw in 1933,
And these guys, broad-

Shouldered like Chicago
Spoke like Manhattan

At 4 am, with a kerchief
Filed with marbles

Whacking a blind
Teller endlessly

While his daughter
Bled out on a wire.

Awful mess.
Tough business, this

Democracy. So the bastards
Were ushered in, even

Though we all knew them
As evil ones, guys

Who hated spics and
Dagos and kikes.

Real Archie Bunkers, to
Be direct. Sort of KKK

Aficionados. Old
School SS-Rottenführers.

Real brown shirt creeps.
They marched into

The best penthouse
Guarded by dump trucks

Filled with sand
In case the so-called towelheads

Attacked, which, to be
Fair, was not a bad idea

In some quarters.
Poets started buying guns

And carrying them
Under their Lorcas.

A billionaire
Party got underway

In several languages,
But the screams

Of the youngest children
In the far room

That was Dostoyevskian,
We were sure of that,

As we applauded
The new bastard-in-chief,

Then slowly backed out,
As if the squeals of that girl

Were not pain, but fun.
It was all ordered,

Transition respected,
So we moved the older

Bastard out, put the new
Bastard in, and then

Prepared for the deluge;
Preparing to call it

Just a bit of rain,
Before the light arcs.

REPLICON

Chords get tangled,
The blue in the offer,

Which was virgin.
I am not a forgetter,

Retain, water-based,
Too much. Complex

Words are only less
Complex words

Engendered. Do you
Endanger new music

When you invariably
Echo Gary Numan?

His chameleons
Bled out colourfield

For me. I saw
In Paris Rothko

And was awedled.
Puns were repellent

Until Bernstein
Said go forth

And Stultify.
Spoonerism anthology

More like. Some Muldoon.
My forebears were

Predatory, T-Rex
Gonged, banged,

Tangled up in tree.
I don't take well

To being called on
To make replies

On the telephone.
They orgied,

Roger that, these
Monogamous poets,

But not monogamous
In less than triplicate;

Coke addled,
Addled Stevenson;

Awfully good to meet
Rothko, in his vast

Sense of pause.
Your numbers,

And a diction of cartography
Is all Nam to me.

I am clicks from base.
It's drones now,

Soon super-
Intelligence.

You will be replaced
By an exact replica

And no one will say
Other than that

At reception. So, no,
I do not totally

Repeat totally
Recall the time we tangoed

In Saigon, with the
Sisters and the blow.

Blowback, eventually,
All wet work has a tongue

And groove network;
And she did kill

The stooge in the photo;
And I was there echo one

Charlie Bravo; but never
Myself, alone, alive-O.

(poem in dialogue with a poem by Aaron Kent)

ON READING DEREK MAHON

I wonder at how often
and when these poems
so well-wrought
will earn the readers

in the coming years
of digital concupiscence
and onanistic thrills.
A Chinese wall

is built around the fire
wall, and that is ringed
by weird indifference
to anything too brilliantly

said. There is a formal
way of being great
that has the fate of being
misunderstood.

Experiment and hate
together pull down
the banners of a kingdom
built on the quaint

ideals of elegance or chivalric
poise. The noise we intake
instead is the bread
of ignorance we break

with ourselves.
Our brains have softened
as our tongues harden;
citadels are closed;

we're bored and boring
in equal measure
unless maintained
at a pitch would kill Darwin

or Churchill; Mahon's
style is beautiful, still, serious,
and makes an occasion
of the flow and spill

of words into a vase; a frame.
There is an object to the art
of poetry, it is that spoken song
in itself is less wrong

than remaining dumb;
no stone is Virgil
on the way to heaven;
one has to burst

into flame or stay a coal;
impacted into a cold potential.
Burn, burn,
and make of the line

a place to raise not decline.
There is the bestial bond
and the civil act;
a poet makes a pact

with savage calm, unruffled
madness squared into a dance
that has its measures
and its chance to obtain

moments of pause and freedom
beyond the domains
where normal countermeasures remain.
So it is I realise, upon reading Mahon,

who knew deep silences of loss
and lost places closest to home
or farthest – sheds, Antarctica, Delft –
contain their cause within the microcosm;

the battles on the plains of Abraham
were also felt in the fleas
on Montcalm's mount,
in the heft of Wolfe's lance; worlds

are less and more in one local fact;
but plain and bare and bald
vocalities are not true to the colours
of any tribal claims.

The bridge
of eloquence
needs to be crossed
more often.

May Sundays
during the afternoons
after Austrian pastries
and coffee with iced cream

and a lack of rain.
Nature is cruel
like a tongue
that speaks its mind.

We need to cross
eloquently
into silence unnerved.
You read to not be dead.

I write and speak. I speak
and am alive.
Words are the leaves
that thrive on sound.

We make the sounds
to bring a speaking sea
to the knowing shore
with the bridge

of our mouths.
In that mouth a tree.
A flowering.
Truth is not what is said.

Truth is the life when speech
is made. Poems are lyrical
even if you hit them with
a lobster hammer.

They make a clearing
in the throat
for something better
than possible to escape.

Poetry is unemployable
nonsense and inescapable
business but it is achievable
knowledge of what is possible.

15 May, 2016
Maida Vale, London

MYSTERIUM PASCHALE

It happens like this
in writing, a man
is brought to a hill to be raised
to die in spring

so that God's will
be done. Never kill alone,
use Romans when you can,
and let care down by a kiss.

I am born in words
and reborn reading; when the ink
from the black well spills.
These trees here are torn

between bliss and dismay, it is confusing
how the world is making progress
even as it staggers back
on one bleakest Saturday;

a chasm opens like a speech
the monster of all creation makes
but that is a volcanic belch
instead; God is dead to live,

the twisting snakery of organised
deception at the tricked hinge
of Easter, where the magic
is love's risk of everything.

But fixed. Stacked. A house
that knows its odds. I never complain
that Christ rises on the Sunday,
it is good theatre and good news.

It is truce with warring nature;
why spar with Caesar forever?
The people who said no
become those who say yes, later.

The mob is just indifferent
ignorance; it gets confused,
as I say, when sung or spoken;
it is a story, not a truth.

It is Truth, happening all at once
and everywhere like a storm
so big it lifts a hemisphere.
I forgive those who hissed and nailed.

Our God was impaled, he suffered
so that God knows what we do
when we die. We are the pain
he endured, unified in injustice.

You ask why discomforts must occur
to be experienced even by God?
A child without water, a desert hot
as coals and no wheat or river there:

the world was made in confusion,
this is certain, it is particularly
creative and dense, and packed
with motion and processions;

never reverses; flows, and alters,
as do minds, and souls. It occurs,
the world, as does a work of art;
it has, even, a sort of heart.

And so, this cannot be stopped,
as one stops a clock to change time.
That would not be freedom, only artifice;
we would be golden statues

in a pearl garden under a jade sky.
No movement and no chance to change
or learn. Dying here is what change
makes happen as its form.

The wind dices for the skein of things
that cannot be rent apart, whole;
ice in the heart of the law
did not even thaw for Jesus.

We have weather even for our God,
one sky, one cruel domain,
it is the same, it is the one that saw
our tender Lord both fall and fly.

Easter Sunday
2016

EVERY ONE BACK THEN

I *still love you* is a lie, and truth,
just as 'Beach House' is a place

and band, and both are slow
in winter, or when winter tries

to address the day in its white tie.
Not much mirth in being bereft;

the heft of what you cannot lift
is the gap between dead and alive,

on those posters; but being wanted
is required. I once knew someone

to say (it was every one back
then in high school, really)

that *indifference is worse*
than hate. An emptiness

on a dinner plate stacks up
against a poisoned chalice

on a tray in a dumb ritual, maybe.
Her name was Ruth, was Fay.

Was Fever. Was Ray. Knife.
Was the king of lies, plus love

in a house of spies. Was Nun
and None and Nin and Sis.

Was adopted daughter, stray.
Darkness on evening's rim.

Sleeping in after an opium craze.
Is lyric a fire a dance a wave

a ripple a spear or a line? Shape
of music in language we adopt

comes cropped by stern disciplines.
I did not know my need for good

or rectitude would shoulder aside
in my vast pride and mean estates

a privilege to look upon, to hold
your kind body again. I said often

you were an evil in my side,
so now I rise alone at night, old,

knowing my greed was imperfect,
your offer impermanent.

DOOMSDAY

(listening to Ryan Adams)

What we wanted we had
what we had we wanted
so why so haunted, so sad?

Better to be glad for what was
then forever after lost,
as if the ship had found

itself aground on shoals of gold;
we sailed to a place far
from the start, which was a port

built from the forests of our heart,
or hearts, plural, for we were two,
and separate, as all persons are,

divisible, as any year,
into the cold and the hotter part;
a recipe for seasonal disaffection,

the falling apart that makes history
never a dull read; we tossed
on a bed we made, that we had,

and wanted, and a bed, moreover
that we had bought on loan
from a miser who called himself

Mr Pound, and kept his love
on a high shelf with his porn;
when young we make our own;

later, the images that return
are erotica from a vintage start;
we ran the four minute mile

in seconds flat, and loved hard
in our rented flat, a squat, a plot,
a bit of all right; we cut the night

into equal episodes of sheer pleasure;
and now, I wake in the dark,
you twenty-five years away

where the ships sank; and the only bank
we owned, the bank of us,
long ago went bust, and yes, speak

of ghosts here, who partook,
and once wore our clothes,
had our lines, deposited our words,

claimed our love; our love was real,
and what is real is there to steal;
it sank, was stolen, the bank of fog

rolled in, like a steamroller,
it was all paved over, the forests
of our desire and satiation;

the nation we founded foundered;
the god we loved dried up into a creek;
it was a river flood, was good;

I sit up in the dark and go for a glass
of London tap; tepid in the half-light,
cock cold and head gin-sagged,

a man who once had a name on his tongue;
never stop being young, cling
to the rotten planks as they toss and turn

in the whirling waters of the maelstrom;
burn and burn for what is spring and spring
in our loins and longing – run to her or him;

and hold on, and hold on. Time is coming
to ruin all your investments and companies;
soon it will gutter and rust, and in trust

will be an ironic echo of a lost promise
in unforgiving lands; please love what is before you;
it is difficult to grow away from being who you were;

we all envy what we were; are identical in time
to the garlanded, running, shining ones
who won the races, kicked off

all traces, and took death
as a joke, in sexual joy
erased sensual fate.

Only love is strong,
strength fades.
Recall, recall.

Then
not
at all.

DREAM-BEAUTY-PSYCHO

(for David Lynch)

Come Lord Jesus
I am unable to love
want sex with porn stars
desire Taylor Swift's fame
my inner life is not my own
I am owned and operated by
digital appearances and offers.
Open my whatever I am into hope
at the ceiling of the lit year be good
allow me to turn from the other paths
offered by hip succubines, Beastians,
all those whose kneeling is for suckery, no
I am sick with using pleasure as a get out clause
I hate my vacuity and eager bingewatching
what new world springs into being with wargames?
I am compromised and have multiple personality
disorders of a spreadeagled self of vapid scrambling selves
no agreements or concords can appease the fly lord now;

no one prays to monsters at the moment of their death.
Jesus of Quebec farmhouses in deep winter I am astray
in a dismaying windblown blinding blizzard without comfort;
my fingers blacken and I lie down a child to sleep forever without pain;
come now and bring me out of howling circles of promised height;
the true path is not a path at all but a carrying over from you to light;
there is no achievement in orgasmic coming at the bleeding of the ewe;
grotesque sacrifice and esoteric coteries send spicules to blind what is right;
corrected vision never requires to see or know; fires are for infernal fans;
we are bathed in a radiation that pierces and blends and sends out rays ahead;
Come Jesus come
and kill my need for porno rhetoric and smartphone desire
for servile she-vamps hissing as they ride my risen king snake.
Words and thoughts commingle with corruption and corrupted things
and all meanings that strive to live above God break the limits for the broken sake;
we only need one obscene transgression for our ritual of adoration
and that was the sex-crime of crucifixion of the great human body which you made us accept.
God in your shocking power are more bloody and weird than the demons that mock you;
but their ejaculating spittle is trivial shame compared to your gross incarnation which appalls
even those who grovel in a rutting pit among the other ways and laws for self and power;
the Lord never denies satisfactions of the uppermost kind
and the laws of love are surprising;

out of the bawling storm, ride! Squall-babe,
on a driving bloody mane, to laugh at them who say
the other ways are most enriched and possess
arcane insights above Christmas;
winter baby blast he and she devils aside and bawl
so brightly of a madder overcoming love of blessing angels.

ON READING DENISE RILEY'S LATEST COLLECTION

I have no business (being an I)
intruding or hiding here.

To conceal is to claim I am
a thing worth keeping from someone

or some thing. Some body.
Bodies are extended metaphors

for extension, just as bank loans
are tropes for needing money.

It is all the same to me.
This landscape is a painting

in a gallery wandered about in
by lawyers here for the wine

and the chance to hit it off
with someone for a variety

of reasons, not one remotely
to do with the art. Which is okay.

Art is hardly interested in them, either.
It is a two-way street, indifference.

Most things remain remote
from the world of other minds;

it is unclear what things feel
about being inhuman, inanimate.

What would they say to Disney
or any two-bit Michelangelo

who might disturb their dull stasis
with reverse mimesis, fantasy?

Guess what? My heart aches
with regards to legal matters

of the head; the hands do cartwheels
on the grass and the brain

half-believes the spirit is the soul
when suddenly, pig's organs

deliver themselves unto our selves
like ripostes from life itself,

a sort of mass-engineered
rollercoaster of the damned

we are strapped into at birth
for the sheer hell of it.

Have no words. For it all.
The colossal shame of death,

the word I thought (I again)
might leave unnamed

as if that would be a defeat
for this non-linear thinker

which is only a disease, a knife,
heroin, a streetcar, a fall, a crate;

thin ice is one skate away
from being a simile for tragedy.

The woodchuck would, but won't.
Quite quaint, working in couplets.

They twin the mirrors they relate.
They spin their tectonic plates

like twins isolate their differences
in subtle acts and ways too shy

to be declaimed or claimed exactly;
a red not blue blouse; a moustache;

well, not that subtle, not too loud.
The cloud of objections to any vehicle

or tenor is diminishing as fewer
comparisons are made.

Quite how it ever got loose is
anybody's guess. Bad luck about

the box, the vase, the lamp, the cage,
whatever broke at this late stage

to let it out to roam at will like words;
the swords of pillage in the early days.

7 June, 2016

LOGAN RECALLED MY FATHER

the night I told you I was smoking junk
and you said that's okay I'm a drunk

was when I most loved you, Dad;
it was in Verdun, at red lights,

dingy snow of March
at the edges of the underpass;

you're as dead as they come;
the time that passed

now is last summer's burnt grass
on lawn after local lawn;

the epic battles of your life
recalled by watching *Logan* –

smaller and less taloned,
but the scars and bearded sorrow,

the once-tall slouch, remind me
my father was strong before

he became weak; and even weak
he worked hard to wade

through waves of shit and mud
to try and rescue his oldest son;

the mind is salvaged if it is
with rusting lines that descend

to haul a wreck halfway up
before a herky-jerky pause

causes commotion on the drifting deck,
tilting in a skewing storm;

those who work to bring the past
to light do no more; films

are improved therapists; in the dark
the screen reveals a bad man being barely

good, running to death to children
in green almost-Canadian woods;

all those blood-stained trees
implying that Eden grows near

to all the wars that came later;
and my father drank and drank,

could be found in a drunk tank;
and I jonesed for no good reasons

beyond wanting to be Coleridge,
which was a misreading of poetry;

and that brief confession in the car
amid the hurt snow

in that littered district of working men
and women, three ten years ago,

well that pitiful union of love
is all I have to show for him now;

and an uncanny mutated man
on the Everyman screen,

ripped open to redeem his crimes
by protecting an abused dark-haired one.

FOR MY WIFE AT SPRING EQUINOX

So, the finest holy music
angels would make
could sound like this: a place
just there, in another room,
someone listening to
Duruflé's Requiem;
and you, human, loving them,
thinking, as if silent air,
that this choir was singing
for both, despite the pain
of everything. Of every
one. Pure noise in the face
of divinest logic, common
as feeling spoken into the rare.

Spring Equinox, 2017

START UP

spring can't be said
without something good happening;
the whole thing speed-ageing; older,
a revolution so natural it looks like
a plan to twist the world asunder,
kicking the heart up to a higher branch;
sun and root power-surging,
as all things should in the annual melee;
postering the way with blossoms
political for the free-way of rain,
in brand new streets, screaming
lead on, go love, go play,
smallest leaflets of rising
ground & sky massively open to changing all.

POEM ON HIS 51ST BIRTHDAY

Because I have to pee
this won't take long;
old men can't fight

but still have their song;
the sun is out,
a small English miracle

during a blackout
of more common sense;
and wars unfurl

like Lear's poor plans,
all news and little peace;
I never have to fake being

in love with the lyrical,
it still has its pull
to and in me; I am not

the man I used to be,
as FYC once said,
but I am at least not dead;

not yet; birthdays age us
conveniently, like genres
in bookshops, arbitrary

and often incomplete,
worse, incompetent.
Do I care if Gary or Lola

recommend Savage Landor
or *Lolita*, or John Green?
I have eaten more chickpeas

than you have ever seen;
this is my day, I declare,
the little prince who adores

FT Prince, as well
as John Ashbery,
though not as much

as I love Grand Master Flash or
Bow Wow Wow; poets need music
in which to grow a separate room,

one less made of smart things;
beauty is mostly the dumbest truths
the loud heart sings;

being is complex, if reflected on,
but refocused on the light
that makes my cat's fur brown.

Being is animal and simple,
mysteriously removed from trouble,
as all napping kittens are;

I am no more a father
than I am a son, now,
but in the absence of paternal

identities can come to love
my Suetonius not as a pet
but gentle equal; though he rivals

my gross affection for food;
lessons to convey to younger readers,
if any I have (and now called fans

or followers on Instagram)?
No lessons, except in poems,
and not even in smart ones;

the word fun is uppermost
in my mind, along with the curse
of wanting to be kind – which hurts

because human laws
too often, in their riptide, lurch
us under to a place of lost decency,

where all struggle after lust and ambition
to reach the air again, the surviving
sky. We sink by definition, being

weighed down by desire; dragged
to the beach, are dried by a rough fire
of driftwood easy to hand,

thrown onto loose sand;
so is our rebirthing pyre unplanned;
I lost my spectacles last year

in Floridian warm water,
shark-infested, within seconds
of rushing into the surf; the waves

smashed me around, threw me
to the anti-surface, and yanked
my seeing-glasses out to depths

that will see them, over eons,
turned to smooth sea-glass, changed
so only green light, and porpoises

can glimpse heaven in their frames;
my name means a bird, or speed;
but turning older is slow, and flightless;

we fly only when we cease
to celebrate the days we came into life;
and birds do not really sing to calendars

of the self-directed mind, but outwards,
like a king so generous with gifts
each daughter has the whole kingdom

to herself, to swing about in, happily.
I like to give with what I have,
which is not sperm, leviathan, or power;

precisely powerless, I fling, instead
the living skein of spidersilk that emits
its transient wirings of vocation

from my prehensile head;
it is called writing, or speaking,
singing, or confession; call it, why not?

a giving of April, of spring, of what comes
next, out of the net of wanting,
into the markets where all goods are free,

and given only out of confusion,
the best kind, between foe and friend,
and what is art & business, work & decency.

8 April, 2017

LEMONADE AND SUNGLASSES, 45 IS A RECORD

'Hey, Hey, Marry Me Archie' – Always

(on my loved one's 45th birthday)

Spring comes in like a loss adjustor
on a bender, slamming down an ice latte
laced with superman-sunshine-butter-gold-stuff;
come see the synagogue, come see the BBC studios;
John Peel was top banana there, he recorded punks, post-
punks and post-post-punks. The second coming of the Jesus
and Mary Chain is the sort of cosmic blunder we must celebrate
with libations, mate. Get a haircut, with a vicious undercut, like Errol
Flynn might've given a pirate in an e.e. cummings poem, had they ever
collaborated. Run for miles in the dazzling midst of unexpected joyousness;
we do not love much these days but chaos that is sliced from the sun, Wallace
S. might have claimed, when dancing around the Floridalicious pouring-outish whack
of a day like this in London, a laudanum and Alternative Ulster moment of pure kicks, roll
that will unearth recently buried Chuck, and throw Bony Moronie out of the media vale prams.

PARIS LOCKED UP

Precisely the incidents
No one will note
In their reports
Saturday in August
Paris locked up
Like all the locksmiths
Who have left the 7th
The wasps gathered by
Cinnamon left out
On a side street
Without qualities
And on Ernest Psichari
Dead silence without
Mourning though the man
Died on this 22nd day
1914
But who remains to recall
A zealot of a Catholic soldier
Who wrote well?
The sound of violent wretching
Rises from the courtyard
As does the sound of power drills
And sanders. Work
Is being done aimlessly
On this sun-blanched day
And no one is serious
Enough to labour or die
Too industriously.
The poems of this moment
Will be few and far

Between. Random if at all
In this more digital age
Of the phone image
Which says it better
And immediately
And goes everywhere
Like a government inspector
Or a phantom or a lie.
I prefer the failed romance
And quaint imperfections
Of the verbal sketch
That can only try
To reach or envisage or contain
Or fetch the altogether
Of its occasions
And which resides
Increasingly in old minds
And disinformed memories
Ancient as the colonel at Alma
Who rode in on his horse
To battle;
And the horse rode out alone
A few minutes later
From the general smoke
And gunnery.

AUTHOR'S END NOTE

Recently, around the time when *Twin Peaks* began again, on 21 May, 2017, I read an article in the *New York Times*, or somewhere else online, reminding us that the series had begun on April 8th, 1990. Now, as it so happens, that date struck a note with me, because that is my birthday, and I turned from 23 to 24 that year, if my arithmetic is correct. 24 is a good year, for most people fortunate to live in North America – I was in Montreal, Canada, and I was madly in love with an American former cheerleader, whose name I will respectfully keep to myself. 1990 was the year my first poetry pamphlet was published, with the help of a good friend, Gordon Buchan. I was, like most people, taken with a few cult shows and films of the time – *Pulp Fiction*, *The X-Files*, and *Twin Peaks*. In some ways, that unholy triumvirate mapped out a post-modern American Gothic, complemented by Pixies, REM, Nirvana and Mazzy Star. America felt dark, expansive, moody, rich and deep, with desire and other primal urges and forces. The supernatural was just around the corner, and might be wearing lipstick. I suppose *The Silence of the Lambs* could be added to this list. Anyway, 27 years later, here is my umpteenth collection – after many full collections published, and, watching the new season it reminded me how much of Kubrick, Welles, and Hitchcock, as well as Dalí, there is in Lynch – but also how much else besides. His *The Elephant Man* remains to me the most terrifyingly moving film ever made, so much so I could not bear to ever watch it again.

   Alone of directors, possibly, Lynch manages to be creepy, subversive, and (at times) deeply empathetic to suffering. Lynch is not a Christian – his monsters are not maybe my monsters, his fears and urges not mine, or his characters' – but he does sense a world of ominous evil all around us, and that is a puritanical vision, on some level. Lynch's high-school gosh sweethearts, and their destruction at the hands of perverts, are both the things of teen dreams, and adult criminal behaviour. His fetishism is made manifest in the name of art. I do not pretend to claim this collection is Lynchian. But few great artists return so fervently, explicitly, and professionally, a quarter of a century later, to a great work, and extend it so magisterially, as Lynch is doing now. Not even Welles made a sequel to *Kane*. The third season of *Twin Peaks* seems to bookend what has been an extraordinary period of Western culture and decline. Lynch has been centrally peripheral all this time, and in some ways, I now suspect, more influential on my imagination, than I might have earlier guessed. Freud and Kafka remain pillars for me, and Poe and Stevens, Yeats and Dickinson – all are reflected in Lynch. Dreams are latent with sex, and death, desire and weirdness. Lynch did not invent psychosis, beauty or dreams, but he has enriched our apprehension of these elements of life experience, in ways that expand aesthetic possibilities – not just for poets or film-makers, or artists, but anyone who has ever wanted to kiss a stranger, on a dark road; or feared doing so. I'd like to subtitle this, poems 1990-2017, but that would be silly – these are poems from 2015 to 2017. But there is an aura here, I now see, an ectoplasm, of the *Twin Peaks* resin, in my work, all along. It may be that growing up in a small town, with lots of fir trees, and facing madness and weirdness early on, I was pre-Lynchian, or co-Lynchian. But anyway, I thought it would be neat to mention this, here, about these poems that tussle with erotic dreams, the desire to be good, and the seeking after meaning in a darkening time.

21 May 2017, London

TODD SWIFT

is the Montreal-born, British
founder-director of Eyewear Publishing,
based in London and now in its 6th year. His own
poems are selected by Salmon in Ireland and Marick
in the USA. He has edited and co-edited over a dozen
anthologies since 1988, including *The Poet's Quest
For God*. His previous book is *Madness & Love In Maida
Vale* (2016). His PhD is from UEA, on style in mid-
century British poets, notably Tiller and Prince. His
essays on poetry have recently appeared in academic
publications from Palgrave and the University of
Liverpool, as well as in *Poetry* magazine and *Poetry
London*. He was included in *The Oxford Companion to
Modern Poetry in English*. He is the
2017/18 Writer-in-residence for Pembroke
College, Cambridge University.